CHRISTMAS
AND MRS HOOPER

A Comedy in One Act for Eight Women
by
L. du GARDE PEACH

SAMUEL   FRENCH

LONDON
NEW YORK   TORONTO   SYDNEY   HOLLYWOOD

Fee for each and every
performance by amateurs   Code C
in the British Isles

CHARACTERS

(in the order of their appearance)

MRS JONES
HILDA
MRS SMALLEY
MRS HOOPER
MRS DEWSBURY
MISS ENDLING
PHYLLIS TATE
MISS WARDLOW

The action of the Play passes in any Village Hall

CHRISTMAS AND MRS HOOPER

SCENE—*Any Village Hall. This means that the play can be acted without a stage or scenery of any kind. All that is necessary are a few chairs. The audience may be seated all round the players; on three sides of them; or grouped at one end of the hall facing them, according to the suitability of the entrances, or the preference of the producer. Throughout the scene the players come in casually and naturally, as they would enter any village hall: they take no notice of the assembled audience.*

MRS WILLOUGHBY-JONES *flutters brightly, determined to make everything go well.* HILDA *is stolid. They arrange the chairs during the opening lines.*

MRS JONES. Now, Hilda, it's nearly time. We'll just set out a few chairs, shall we?

HILDA. How many, mum?

MRS JONES. Let me see—six. Yes—six will be enough. Or say, seven. In a sort of circle—with one facing the others.

HILDA. If it's a circle everybody's facing.

MRS JONES (*with a little laugh*) Yes, they are, aren't they? I see you remember your geometry, Hilda. A circle is the shortest distance between two points, and so on. (*Pleasantly*) Don't scrape them on the floor, Hilda. Lift them. That's better.

HILDA. Will them do?

MRS JONES (*correcting her*) *Those*, Hilda.

HILDA. That's right, mum—them.

MRS JONES. *Them* should be *those*, Hilda.

HILDA. Them *is* those.

MRS JONES. Oh well, never mind. Yes—those will do nicely.

HILDA. How many's coming, mum?

MRS JONES (*pleasantly*) Now think, Hilda. **One chair is** for me, and there are six others.

HILDA (*brightly*) Six, mum.

MRS JONES. That's right. You see? You only have to think, don't you?

HILDA (*stolidly*) Yes, mum. (*Looking at the chairs*) Is it sewing?

MRS JONES. No, Hilda. Not sewing—singing.

HILDA (*incredulously*) Singing? Who'll it be?

MRS JONES. Well, of course, I don't know whether they'll all *come*, but I've asked Mrs Smalley and Mrs Dewsbury . . .

HILDA (*even more incredulously*) Mrs *Dewsbury?*

MRS JONES. I'm sure Mrs Dewbury can sing quite nicely.

HILDA. She can't hardly breathe, never mind sing.

MRS JONES (*brightly*) Well, we shall find out, shan't we? Then there's Miss Wardlow and Miss Endling . . .

HILDA. Is them two going to sing?

MRS JONES (*gently reproving her*) Hilda.

HILDA. What? (*Realizing*) Oh—is it grammar?

MRS JONES. There—you see? You know really, don't you? *Those* two, Hilda—not them two.

HILDA (*stolidly*) Yes, mum.

MRS JONES (*brightly*) Now we'll say it again, shall we? Then we'll remember it. What was it? Now careful, Hilda.

HILDA. Is *those* two going to sing?

MRS JONES (*brightly helpful*) Now, Hilda. Think again. Miss Wardlow and Miss Endling are plural, you know.

HILDA (*agreeing*) They are, that—both of 'em!

MRS JONES. So it would be *are*, not *is*, wouldn't it?

HILDA. Yes, mum.

MRS JONES (*brightly encouraging*) Now just *once* more, Hilda?

(HILDA *takes a deep breath, bored but wearily co-operative*)

HILDA. Are them two going to sing?

MRS JONES (*sighing*) Oh well—perhaps we'd better—another time, Hilda.

HILDA (*relieved*) Yes, mum.

MRS JONES. Now where were we? (*Repeating quickly*) Mrs Smalley, Mrs Dewsbury, Miss Wardlow, Miss Endling and—oh, yes—Mrs Hooper . . .

HILDA (*staring*) Not Mrs *Hooper*, mum?

MRS JONES (*smiling a little dubiously*) I hope Mrs Hooper will come.

HILDA (*as though unable to believe it*) Singing?

MRS JONES. Mrs Hooper will—well, if she sings with the others perhaps she won't be heard too much.

HILDA (*with conviction*) *They* won't, you mean. Mrs Hooper's got a voice like one of them things—(*correcting herself with a glance at Mrs Jones*)—*those* things—what they dig up roads with.

MRS JONES (*sighing in spite of herself*) I know, Hilda. But Mrs Hooper gets so upset if she's left *out* of anything.

HILDA. That's right, mum. Nosey—that's what she is.

MRS JONES. No—no, Hilda. Interested. And, of course, she can't help her voice, can she? It's—it's asthma.

HILDA. It's *beer*.

(MRS JONES *gives a little laugh, determined to be bright, and flutteringly anxious to avoid any unpleasantness, even with Hilda*)

MRS JONES. Well, shall we say perhaps a little of both. There—that's all, I think—though I *did* mention to Phyllis Tate that perhaps . . . But, of course, she may not come.

HILDA. She's all right, isn't she, mum? Them others don't like her, though. Jealous, that's what they are.

MRS JONES. Oh, no, Hilda—I'm sure they're not. Miss Endling . . .

HILDA (*enthusiastically*) Hasn't she got lovely legs?

MRS JONES (*surprised*) Miss Endling?

HILDA (*with a little splutter of laughter*) Eeeh, no—Phyllis Tate. Lovely, they are!

MRS JONES (*disapprovingly*) Yes—I'm sure Phyllis Tate is very—well, nicely made.

HILDA. She is, that. (*Enviously*) I wish I'd got legs like them what she's got.

MRS JONES (*sadly*) Oh, dear, Hilda. I'm afraid I shall never teach you the difference between *them* and *those*.

HILDA. No, mum. (*With a bright smile*) It's uphill work, isn't it, mum?

MRS JONES (*brightly*) Never mind, Hilda. If at first you don't succeed, you know . . .

HILDA. I know, mum—keep on nagging.

(MRS SMALLEY *comes in. She is a little body with a happy gift for enjoying other people's misfortunes. Her bright eyes miss nothing*)

MRS JONES. Come in, Mrs Smalley. First as usual.

MRS SMALLEY. I don't hang about like some. Get on with it—that's my motto. Always was. Chairs for six, I see. Is it the usual?

MRS JONES. You mean . . .

MRS SMALLEY. I mean is it them as usually comes?

HILDA (*rapidly—all in one breath*) Mrs Dewsbury, Mrs Hooper, Miss Wardlow, Miss Endling, and her with them lovely legs.

MRS JONES. That'll do, Hilda.

MRS SMALLEY (*disapprovingly*) Did you say legs?

MRS JONES (*with a nervous laugh*) Hilda meant—er— Phyllis Tate, you know. She thinks her—lower extremities —are—er . . .

MRS SMALLEY (*with a strongly disapproving sniff*) She might well, after that panto as they had last Christmas. I hope as there isn't going to be nothing of the sort *this* Christmas. I haven't hardly got over it yet.

HILDA (*under her breath*) I'll bet you haven't.

MRS JONES (*warningly*) Hilda. (*To Mrs Smalley. Brightly*) Of course it was popular, wasn't it? Everybody liked it.

MRS SMALLEY. *Some* did!

MRS JONES. But I'm afraid we couldn't do anything like that, you know.

MRS SMALLEY. Nor want to!

MRS JONES. So I thought something with a real Christmas atmosphere . . .

MRS SMALLEY (*suspiciously*) Such as?

MRS JONES (*fluttering*) Now you're going to be surprised at this, Mrs Smalley.

MRS SMALLEY. It takes a lot to surprise me, mum, after what I've been through. If I was to tell you . . .

MRS JONES (*hastily*) Yes, I'm sure you have, Mrs Smalley.

MRS SMALLEY. Have I ever told you about my operation?

HILDA. You've told everybody.

MRS SMALLEY (*severely*) I don't know as I was addressing you, young woman.

MRS JONES. That'll do, Hilda.

HILDA (*stolidly*) Yes'm. But if she starts . . .

MRS JONES (*patiently—not sharply*) Hilda.

(MRS HOOPER *enters. She is an aggressive type, loud and notably lacking in tact*)

MRS SMALLEY. I don't know what young people's coming to and that's a fact. When I was a girl . . .

MRS HOOPER. Oh—ancient history, is it?

MRS SMALLEY. No, it isn't. And if you want to . . .

MRS JONES (*interposing hurriedly*) Come in, Mrs Hooper. So nice of you to come.

MRS HOOPER. I haven't much time, but seeing as how I was invited . . .

MRS JONES. Of course you were, Mrs Hooper. We shouldn't dream of leaving you out.

MRS HOOPER. What of?

MRS JONES. Well, as I was just telling Mrs Smalley when you came in . . .

MRS HOOPER. Trust Jane Smalley to be first, if it's something for nothing.

MRS JONES (*not understanding*) Yes, we're all of us ready to do our bit, without hope of reward—on earth, that is. As the Vicar used to say . . .

MRS SMALLEY (*to Mrs Hooper*) I don't know as I've seen *you* here since they was giving away the remains of the Harvest Festival.

MRS JONES. Yes, Mrs Hooper's always ready to help—clearing up, and so on.

HILDA. She is that!

MRS HOOPER (*turning on her*) What was that?

HILDA (*with spirit*) Who was it got away with the big marrow and all them grapes?

MRS JONES (*automatically*) *Those* grapes. (*Realizing*) No —no. That will *do*, Hilda.

MRS HOOPER. Was I given them, or wasn't I?

MRS SMALLEY. You wasn't!

MRS JONES. *Please*, Mrs Hooper.

Mrs Hooper. It's all very well—please. It's what I expect from Jane Smalley. But as for you, my girl, I don't know what young people's coming to.

Hilda (*cheekily*) That's two of you doesn't, does you?

Mrs Jones (*quite sharply for her*) Hilda!

Mrs Hooper. Back answers—so that's what it's come to. Back answers! To *me*, that's brought up nine!

Hilda. I wasn't one of 'em!

Mrs Hooper. Lucky for you. If you had been . . .

Mrs Jones (*hastily*) I'm sure you're a wonderful mother, Mrs Hooper—quite wonderful . . .

Mrs Hooper. I did what was right by them, that I *will* say. They never lacked clouting.

Mrs Jones (*fatuously*) No, I'm sure you gave them lots of everything. But—(*with a little laugh*)—that isn't what we're here for, is it? Very interesting, of course, but . . .

Mrs Hooper. And what *are* we here for, if it's not asking too much?

Mrs Jones. Oh, no, Mrs Hooper. Not at all. Of course —I mean, now you're here you want to know, don't you?

Mrs Smalley. All I can say is, I hope as it's something respectable.

Mrs Jones. Oh, it is. In fact . . .

(Mrs Dewsbury, *fat and stupid*, and Miss Endling, *an acidulated spinster, wearing pince-nez, enter*)

Oh, do come in, Mrs Dewsbury. And Miss Endling. Now isn't that nice. Quite a little gathering.

Mrs Dewsbury. I nearly didn't come. I don't get about like I did. It's me breath.

Miss Endling. How are you, dear Mrs Willoughby-Jones. So sweet of you to ask me to—whatever it is.

Mrs Jones. Oh, no, dear. It's very kind of you. You know Mrs Hooper and Mrs Smalley.

Miss Endling (*peering at them short-sightedly*) I do. (*Without enthusiasm*) How do you do?

Mrs Smalley (*acidly*) Quite well, I'm sure, and thank you for asking.

Mrs Hooper (*aggressively*) Blooming—that's what I am, blooming. *And* ready for anything.

Mrs Jones (*fussily*) Yes, of course, you always were, weren't you, Mrs Hooper. So very—helpful, and—er—(*more faintly*)—helpful.

Mrs Hooper. Always ready to give an 'elping 'and—if I know what the 'elping 'and's 'elping, as you might say. What would it be this time?

Mrs Jones. Now that we're all here—well, nearly all . . .

Mrs Dewsbury. Is there more coming?

Mrs Jones. Miss Wardlow . . .

Mrs Hooper (*scornfully*) Oh, her!

Mrs Jones. She's a very good worker.

Mrs Hooper. Can't say boo to a goose. Any more?

Mrs Jones (*diffidently*) I *did* ask Phyllis Tate—but, of course—young people these days . . .

Mrs Hooper. When last seen, endangering the public in a blue streak on four wheels.

Miss Endling. That girl ought not to be allowed to drive a car, in my opinion.

Mrs Hooper. It'd do *her* good to be pushing a pram.

(Phyllis Tate—*a pretty girl of about nineteen, dressed in slacks and a duffel coat*—enters, followed by Miss Wardlow. *Miss Wardlow is mouse-like and pours oil on any troubled waters that may be going*)

Mrs Jones. She has a good heart.

Hilda. And lovely legs!

Phyllis (*cheerfully*) Sounds as though you were talking about me. Hallo, everybody.

Mrs Jones. Oh, there you are, dear. I was afraid that perhaps you might not be able to—how are you, Miss Wardlow? So nice of you to come.

Miss Wardlow. I'm afraid I shan't be much use, you know, but anything I can do . . .

Mrs Hooper. You don't know what it is, yet.

Miss Wardlow. Whatever it is, really.

Phyllis. Rot. You're a tower of strength, Miss Wardlow.

Miss Wardlow. Oh, no, dear. (*To Mrs Jones*) I'm sorry if I'm late. I shouldn't have been here at all if Phyllis hadn't picked me up.

PHYLLIS (*laughing*)   *And* scared the daylight out you, eh?

MISS WARDLOW.   I think you're a very good driver.

PHYLLIS.   I shouldn't be here if I weren't, should I, Miss Endling?

MISS ENDLING (*acidly*)   I agree with Mrs Hooper.

PHYLLIS (*surprised*)   That's something new.

MRS HOOPER.   You're a danger to the public, young woman.

PHYLLIS.   Only the male half of it. (*To Mrs Jones*) Is everybody here?

MRS JONES.   Yes—yes, I think everybody's here now. I thought it was better not to ask any men.

PHYLLIS.   It depends what for, doesn't it. Well? Shall we get cracking? What is it, by the way?

(MRS JONES *looks round with a diffident but hopeful smile*)

MRS JONES.   Well—seeing that it will soon be Christmas . . .

MRS HOOPER.   It will. *And* I reckon nothing to it, neither.

MRS JONES (*taken aback*)   Nothing? Oh, but surely, Mrs Hooper—Christmas!

MRS HOOPER.   If you'd nine to do for—not counting Hooper—and all of 'em expecting Christmas dinners as no Christian didn't ought to be expected to provide not for nobody.

MRS SMALLEY.   That's right.

MISS WARDLOW.   Oh, but I'm sure your cooking is wonderful, Mrs Hooper.

MRS HOOPER (*aggressively*)   I'm not saying it isn't, am I?

MISS WARDLOW (*hurriedly*)   Oh, no—no. Nobody is. I mean—that's why they want so much. Mince-pies and so on . . .

MRS HOOPER.   They'd be lucky! One pudding I'll make, I say, and no more. Like it or leave it, I say.

PHYLLIS.   And what's the betting?

MRS HOOPER.   Never mind betting. My pudding's is 'et —to the last crumb.

MRS JONES.   To the last crumb! Isn't that nice? Of course, I was just going to explain . . .

PHYLLIS.   *Sorry.* Hold it, everybody.

MRS JONES (*again looking round her with a brightly wistful smile*) Well—I thought that . . .

MRS DEWSBURY (*suddenly*) Peace on earth, goodwill to man.

(*They all turn and look at her*)

That's what I say Christmas is.

MRS JONES. Of course, Mrs Dewsbury. We all . . .

MRS DEWSBURY (*firmly*) Peace on earth, goodwill to man. I've said that ever since I was a girl, I've said it.

MRS HOOPER. What about acting on it?

MRS DEWSBURY. If you was half the Christian what I am, Alice Hooper, you'd have reason to talk.

MRS HOOPER. And if you'd brought up nine, not counting Hooper—him being my third . . .

MRS JONES (*interposing*) Yes, of course, Mrs Hooper. Such sweet little boys.

MRS HOOPER (*staring in surprise*) Sweet? Them little devils?

MRS JONES (*flustered*) Oh, but Mrs Hooper—your own children . . .

MRS HOOPER. If they was to hear you call 'em sweet, mum, you wouldn't have a window left not broke!

MISS ENDLING. Disgraceful!

MRS HOOPER (*turning on her*) Wait while you've had nine —*you'll* see!

MRS SMALLEY. Some hopes!

MISS ENDLING (*sharply*) What was that?

MRS JONES. Mrs Smalley meant while there's life there's hope, didn't you, Mrs Smalley?

MRS SMALLEY. I didn't.

MRS JONES (*fatuously*) Yes, of course. But we aren't getting on, are we?

PHYLLIS. Actually, I'm enjoying every minute of it.

MRS JONES. I'm so glad, dear. But I really think I ought to explain what we've come for, you know.

MRS HOOPER. 'Sright. We haven't all day.

MISS WARDLOW. I'm sure we're all very ready to help.

MRS JONES. Thank you, dear. Well—(*looking round, smiling hopefully*)—it's carols.

(*There is a moment's silence while they take it in*)

MRS HOOPER. You mean singing?

MRS JONES. Yes. Carol singing.

MISS WARDLOW. Such a nice idea. I'll do my best, of course, but I'm afraid my voice isn't very . . .

MRS HOOPER (*interrupting*) Mine *is*. A little lark—that's what 'Arbottle used to say—he was my second—a little lark!

MRS SMALLEY. Some lark!

MRS HOOPER. Everybody what heard it said the same. And if you're jealous, Jane Smalley, you needn't show it so plain. I used to keep the whole street happy.

MRS SMALLEY. Awake, you mean.

MRS JONES. I'm sure you did, Mrs Hooper.

PHYLLIS. Actually my voice would stop a clock, but I'm game.

MRS DEWSBURY. I don't know about singing. It's me breath.

MRS JONES. We know you'll do your best, Mrs Dewsbury. And, of course, Miss Endling's quite a vocalist . . .

MISS ENDLING (*with a modest smirk*) I used to entertain the soldiers during the war.

MRS HOOPER. What war?

MISS ENDLING (*sharply*) The last war. I was quite a girl, of course.

MRS HOOPER (*aside, to Mrs Smalley*) Crimea.

MISS ENDLING. What was that?

MRS JONES. Mrs Hooper will have her little joke, won't you, Mrs Hooper? (*With an unconvincing little laugh*) Ha, ha. Very amusing. What about you, Mrs Smalley?

MRS SMALLEY. Eh, I haven't sung since who will o'er the downs so free at the school concert.

MRS HOOPER. I remember that one. (*Quoting*) Oh, who will up and follow me to win a blooming bride.

MRS JONES (*flustered*) Yes, of course, Mrs Hooper. But there are—well—some expressions which we try not to use at our little meetings, aren't there?

PHYLLIS (*amused*) That's all right. It's in the song. It means the bride was blooming—not a blooming bride— as you might say a blooming nuisance.

MRS JONES (*gently*) Only you wouldn't, would you, dear?

MRS HOOPER. She wouldn't! I know what *she'd* say.

PHYLLIS. Good for you.

MRS JONES (*a little anxiously*) Yes—well, shall we get on?

MISS WARDLOW (*helpfully*) I'm sure we'd all like to know more.

MRS JONES. Thank you, dear. I thought *Good King Wenceslas*. I've got the words here, and of course we all know the tune. (*She hands a sheet of paper to each of them*)

(*They look at it*—MRS HOOPER, MRS SMALLEY, *and* MRS DEWSBURY *somewhat dubiously*)

HILDA. What about me?

MRS JONES. Of course, Hilda—you can have mine.

HILDA. If I'm not wanted . . .

MRS JONES (*gently*) Now, Hilda. I'm sure you sing very nicely.

HILDA. I got a prize for it—which is more than some.

MRS HOOPER (*looking at the paper*) Well—fancy that!

MRS JONES (*anxiously*) What is it, Mrs Hooper?

MRS HOOPER. All them verses. I never knew as there was more than one.

MRS JONES. Oh, yes—it's a little story. The good king and the poor man . . .

MRS HOOPER. Not when I've heard it, it hasn't been. It's Hooper. He always goes to the door half-way through the first verse when them boys come singing it. They never get no further.

MRS JONES. You mean he gives them something.

MRS HOOPER. He tells 'em what he *will* give 'em, if they don't 'op it. Eh—the things he says! Laugh!

MRS JONES. Not a very Christian spirit.

MRS HOOPER (*cheerfully*) If you'd lived with Hooper as long as what I have, you'd know as there wasn't nothing Christian about *him*. Of course, him being in the coal business you couldn't hardly expect it, could you? What I say is . . .

MISS ENDLING (*impatiently*) *Could* we get on—because if not . . .

MRS JONES. Yes, of course. (*To Mrs Hooper*) Another

time, Mrs Hooper, shall we? Perhaps we'd better start a
little—well, rehearsal, really. Now if I give you a note . . .
(*She hums a note*)

MRS SMALLEY. Where was he king of?

MRS JONES (*pausing*) What was that, Mrs Smalley?

MRS SMALLEY. Wenceslas. Where was he king of?

MRS DEWSBURY. England.

MISS ENDLING. Nonsense.

MRS DEWSBURY. It's all right—nonsense. I did my history same as anybody else. He was before King Alfred and
Henry VIII.

MISS WARDLOW (*gently*) If he was before King Alfred he
would have to be before Henry VIII, wouldn't he?

MRS DEWSBURY. That's what I said.

MRS SMALLEY. You said he was before both of 'em.

MISS ENDLING. Rubbish. He wasn't anything of the sort.

MRS DEWSBURY. Who was he before, then?

MISS ENDLING. He wasn't an English king at all.

PHYLLIS. What about Russia?

MRS JONES. Oh, no, dear—not Russia. People get so
upset when it's mentioned.

MRS HOOPER. And rightly. If you ask me, they're nothing but a lot of Bolshies, them Russians. You should hear
what Hooper says about 'em.

PHYLLIS. I should love to.

MRS JONES. No, Phyllis—please. (*To Mrs Smalley*) Of
course it doesn't say in the carol where he was king of, so
perhaps we'd better just leave it, shall we?

MRS SMALLEY. I was only asking.

MRS JONES. Quite right, Mrs Smalley. I'm sure it would
be very interesting if we knew. But as the Vicar used to say,
there are things that are hidden from us. Now, shall we
try the first verse?

PHYLLIS. O.K. by me. I couldn't care less if he was king
of the Cannibal Islands.

MISS ENDLING. He wasn't.

MRS HOOPER. How do *you* know? If you don't know
where he was king of, you don't know where he wasn't.

MRS JONES. Quite right, Mrs Hooper. (*Cheerfully*) That
settles it, of course. Now shall we . . .

MISS ENDLING. It does nothing of the sort.

MISS WARDLOW (*soothingly*) Couldn't we just take it that he was king of somewhere unnamed?

MRS SMALLEY. It wasn't one of them hot countries—not with all that snow about.

MRS JONES (*fatuously*) Thank you, Mrs Smalley. A very good suggestion. Now—I'll give a note, shall I? (*Humming a note*) Now—all together.

(*They sing the first verse of "Wenceslas" to the best of their ability*)

Very nice. Really, there's nothing quite like singing a carol together, is there?

PHYLLIS. Nothing—fortunately!

MRS HOOPER. If you ask me, it doesn't make sense, gathering winter fuel with snow all over.

MRS DEWSBURY. It does seem like he'd left it a bit late.

MRS HOOPER. Late? He wouldn't get any—not if the snow was deep like it says.

MRS SMALLEY. He was pinching it.

MRS JONES. Oh, no, Mrs Smalley—not in a carol.

MRS SMALLEY. Why was he getting it at night, then? It says brightly shone the moon that night.

MRS HOOPER. 'Sright. He was one of them luneys. If he wasn't, he'd have got it before the snow come, and if he was pinching it, he'd have gone on a dark night, not when the moon was shining.

MISS WARDLOW. Oh, but the good king wouldn't have helped him, would he, if he had been?

PHYLLIS. You never know, with kings. A queer lot, some of them.

MRS JONES (*gently reproving*) Oh, no, dear, not kings. (*Brightly*) Now that we've settled about the poor man, shall we go on?

MISS ENDLING. It's the king next. Is that to be a solo?

MRS JONES. Oh—I hadn't thought about that.

PHYLLIS. Bit awkward, without a man. I could get you one or two.

MRS SMALLEY. I've no doubt.

PHYLLIS (*grinning*) Or what about Hooper? He's an expert on winter fuel.

MRS JONES (*hurriedly*) Oh, no, Phyllis—*please*.

MRS HOOPER. And why not? Not but what he wouldn't be mixed up in it, not if you paid him, he wouldn't.

MRS JONES (*relieved*) Of course, that settles it, doesn't it? I'm sure that one of us . . .

(*Suddenly* MRS HOOPER *sings the next four lines in a raucous voice*)

MRS HOOPER (*pleased with herself*) What about that?

MRS JONES (*doing her best to be tactful*) Well—it—it was—*different*—wasn't it?

MISS ENDLING. Personally, I think it was awful.

MRS SMALLEY. *And* me.

MRS HOOPER (*to Miss Endling*) Oh, you do? Perhaps you could do it better yourself?

MISS ENDLING. I am a soprano, as everybody knows. (*To Mrs Jones—with a coy expression*) I thought perhaps—if you have no-one in mind for the page—it needs a young voice . . .

MRS HOOPER (*scornfully*) Ha!

MISS ENDLING (*sharply*) And what might you mean by that?

MRS JONES. It was—well—encouragement—wasn't it, Mrs Hooper? (*To Miss Endling*) You see? Mrs Hooper agrees. We should all like to hear you sing. Such a nice idea.

MISS ENDLING. Of course, I'm out of practice.

MRS JONES. Between friends, you know.

MRS HOOPER. Am I to be the king or am I not? That's what I want to know. Because if not I've plenty to do.

MRS JONES (*fluttering*) Oh, yes—we all know how busy you are, Mrs Hooper. In fact, I don't know how you find the time . . .

MRS HOOPER. Am I or am I not. That's all I want to know. Am I or am I not?

MRS SMALLEY. You are not.

MRS HOOPER. I don't know as it's any concern of yours, Jane Smalley. (*To Mrs Jones*) That's all I want to know. Am I or am I not . . .

MRS JONES. Yes, you said so, didn't you. Perhaps if we —I mean—we really ought to hear all the voices and then decide, don't you think?

MRS HOOPER. If there's any more penetrating than what mine is . . .

PHYLLIS. There couldn't be. I vote for Mrs Hooper for the king.

MRS JONES. Oh, do you think so, dear?

PHYLLIS. Volume—that's what the king wants. Something like a jet plane warming up. Well—Mrs Hooper's got it. No, really, Mrs Hooper, I congratulate you. It was terrific. You're in, Mrs Hooper. And with Miss Endling for the page it'll be a wow! Come on, Miss Endling. Don't be shy.

MISS ENDLING (*indignantly*) I am not shy.

PHYLLIS. That's the stuff. Now then—on the beat . . .

(MRS DEWSBURY *has been studying her paper of the words during the above*)

MRS DEWSBURY. It doesn't seem like there was any drifting.

PHYLLIS. What?

MRS DEWSBURY. No drifting. It says the snow was deep and crisp and even. If it was even, there wasn't no drifting.

MRS SMALLEY. No wind.

MRS DEWSBURY. That's what *I* thought.

MRS HOOPER. Talk about snow drifting! Winter before last—or was it the one before that?

MRS JONES. Yes, Mrs Hooper—I'm sure it was. But perhaps—don't you think . . .

PHYLLIS. What does it matter, anyway?

MRS DEWSBURY. If there wasn't no drifting . . .

PHYLLIS. There wasn't. So what? This is a song, not a meteoro discussion—whatever the word is.

MRS HOOPER. It seems to me like you're taking a lot on yourself, young woman.

PHYLLIS (*cheerfully*) Somebody's got to. Now Miss Endling—what about the page?

MISS ENDLING (*acidly*) If everybody's finished interrupting.

MRS DEWSBURY. I was only making a suggestion.

MRS JONES. Yes—very helpful. Thank you, Mrs Dewsbury. Now I'm sure we all want to hear Miss Endling. So if you don't mind, dear . . .

MISS ENDLING. I'm quite ready to do what I can. Of course, I am out of training . . .

MRS JONES. I'm sure a voice like yours doesn't—well—deteriorate, does it?

MISS ENDLING. I hope not. If you wouldn't mind giving me a note . . .

PHYLLIS (*singing*) Tra-la-la-la! There you are. Now—one, two, three . . .

(MISS ENDLING *sings the next four lines wildly out of tune, and changing the key in the middle. As she concludes there is a stunned silence*)

MISS ENDLING (*modestly self-satisfied*) Of course I am a little out of practice.

PHYLLIS. You've said it!

MRS HOOPER. If you ask me . . .

MRS JONES (*hurriedly*) No, Mrs Hooper—please.

MRS HOOPER. All I was going to say, ma'am, is I never heard nothing like it—never!

PHYLLIS. It *was* a bit third programme.

MISS ENDLING (*bristling*) If you're suggesting . . .

MRS SMALLEY. There's them as can sing, and there's them as can't.

MISS ENDLING. Meaning . . . ?

MRS JONES (*distressed*) Oh, dear! *Please*, Mrs Smalley.

PHYLLIS. Look—it's no good beating about the bush. That was a wash-out, Miss Endling. Not your fault . . .

MISS ENDLING. Oh, it was? I'll have you know, young woman, that I've sung at the concerts of the Vegetarian Section of the Fresh Air League.

PHYLLIS (*unruffled*) I dare say vegetarians are different. They can take it.

MRS JONES. Phyllis—please don't say anything to upset Miss Endling.

MISS ENDLING. I am not upset. I have no objection to honest criticism, but when it comes to insults from ignorant women and children——

MRS HOOPER (*aggressively*) Meaning me?

MISS ENDLING. —I prefer to go where my singing is appreciated. (*Firmly*) No. I'm sorry. There are limits to my forbearance. I must ask you to excuse me.

MRS JONES. Oh, please don't go, Miss Endling. I'm sure Phyllis only meant . . .

PHYLLIS. Take it easy, Miss Endling.

MISS ENDLING. I do not propose to take it easy, as you call it. I'm sorry. I'll say good afternoon, Mrs Willoughby-Jones.

MISS WARDLOW (*feebly*) Perhaps if Miss Endling had a little practice . . .

MISS ENDLING. I do not need practice . . .

✗ MRS DEWSBURY (*kindly*) Perhaps if you was to gargle . . .

MRS HOOPER (*enjoying it*) What with? Carbolic?

MISS ENDLING (*with cold dignity*) I'm sorry, Mrs Willoughby-Jones.

MRS JONES (*distressed*) *Must* you go, dear?

MISS ENDLING. I have no alternative. I shall be delighted to come back, any time—when you are *alone*.

(MISS ENDLING *sweeps out*)

MRS JONES. Oh dear, I'm very sorry that should have happened. Miss Endling is so—so . . .

PHYLLIS. So what?

MRS JONES. Helpful, really—well, mostly.

MRS HOOPER. Don't you worry, ma'am. A voice like that isn't no loss. Now if it had been me . . .

PHYLLIS. Cheer up—and look, I've got an idea. What this carol wants is pop.

MRS JONES (*distressed and confused*) Pop?

PHYLLIS. That's right—pop. What about it? I'll show you how to put the page over. (*She jumps up and sings the four lines in pop rhythm, twisting and writhing in imitation of the more extreme pop singers*)

(MRS HOOPER *and* MRS DEWSBURY *thoroughly enjoy it, and applaud.* MRS SMALLEY'S *expression is one of strong disapproval.* MRS JONES *and* MISS WARDLOW *stare in bewilderment*)

MRS HOOPER. Eh, that's the stuff! I haven't enjoyed anything so much since Hooper sat on the gas stove.

PHYLLIS (*flushed and excited*) How about it?

MRS JONES (*dubiously*) Well, dear—I'm not sure it's *quite* what was intended.

MRS SMALLEY. I should think not indeed!

PHYLLIS. This is the jet age. Things have got to *move*. Hot it up! What do you say, Mrs Dewsbury?

MRS DEWSBURY. Eh, lovely! As good as the telly.

PHYLLIS (*triumphantly*) There you are, you see? Mrs Hooper and Mrs Dewsbury are the great British public. Aren't you, Mrs Hooper?

MRS HOOPER. We are, that! (*Getting up*) What about me doing the king with a bit o' pop?

MRS JONES (*hurriedly*) No, Mrs Hooper—no, really. The king has got to have—well, dignity, you know. The way you did it was—(*faintly*)—very nice.

PHYLLIS. I agree Mrs Hooper. Dignity for the king. O.K. for the page, though, eh?

MRS JONES. Well no, dear—I'm afraid that—after all, carols are in a way *religious*, aren't they? (*Hurriedly*) It's very good of you, of course, and I'm sure you meant well . . .

PHYLLIS (*cheerfully*) O.K. Just a suggestion.

MRS JONES (*anxiously*) You don't *mind*, dear, do you?

PHYLLIS. Good lord, no! I'm not Miss Endling. Well? What do we do now? Mrs Dewsbury would do all right for the next verse—I dare say the page would be pretty well gasping after that walk in the snow. But he'd never *start* if he was short of breath to begin with.

MRS DEWSBURY. You're right—it's me breath. It isn't what it used to be.

MRS JONES. Never mind, Mrs Dewsbury—other things make up for it.

MRS HOOPER. What things?

PHYLLIS (*breezily*) Skipping that, if you don't mind, Mrs Hooper—what about Mrs Smalley?

MRS SMALLEY (*primly*) I'd rather not be mixed up in it.

PHYLLIS. Honestly, Mrs Smalley, I don't know how you find time not to be mixed up in so many things. That leaves you, Miss Wardlow.

MISS WARDLOW (*distressed*) Oh, no—please—I couldn't. *Really*, I couldn't.

PHYLLIS. O.K. Then we're back to me. Tough luck, but there it is.

HILDA. What about me?

PHYLLIS. Hilda—of *course!* Good for you.

HILDA. I was the page when we done it at school.

MRS JONES. When you *did* it, Hilda.

HILDA. That's right, mum.

PHYLLIS. Splendid. What about doing it now?

HILDA. I don't mind.

PHYLLIS. Off you go, then. (*She hums a note*) Now—one, two, three.

(HILDA *sings the four lines beginning "Sire, he lives", quite accurately and sweetly*)

MRS JONES. Very good, Hilda. I'd no idea ...

PHYLLIS. You're in, Hilda. Now, Mrs Hooper—the king.

MRS HOOPER. Is it me, again?

PHYLLIS. Yes.

MRS JONES (*nervously*) Oh—do you think ... ?

MRS HOOPER. Don't worry, ma'am. I've made plaster fall off the ceiling before now.

MRS DEWSBURY (*looking at her paper*) What's a league?

PHYLLIS. What did you say?

MRS DEWSBURY. What's a league?

MRS SMALLEY. Tottenham Hotspurs—Wolverhampton Wanderers—Woolwich ...

MRS DEWSBURY. Not that sort. It says, sire, he lives a good league hence.

PHYLLIS. Three miles, isn't it?

MRS DEWSBURY (*triumphantly*) Then if he lived right against the forest fence, like it says, why did he have to go three miles to get his winter fuel—never mind the snow? He only had to nip over the fence to get all he wanted.

MRS HOOPER. He wasn't right, that's why. In his head, I mean.

PHYLLIS. That's a point, certainly. (*To Mrs Jones*) Why did he?

MRS JONES (*flustered*) I've no idea. I never thought about it.

MISS WARDLOW. Perhaps the forest—over the fence, you know—belonged to somebody else.

MRS SMALLEY. He was pinching it. That's why he couldn't do it near where he lived. Like them burglers. They never do it near home.

PHYLLIS. The whole thing sounds pretty bogus to me.

MRS JONES. But if that's how it *happened*, dear . . .

PHYLLIS. Not that it matters. I don't suppose anybody listens to the words.

MRS SMALLEY. It's to be hoped as they don't listen to the tune, neither—not with Alice Hooper singing.

PHYLLIS. People put up with a lot at Christmas.

MRS HOOPER (*aggressively*) Oh, they do?

PHYLLIS. Fortunately. Now come on, Mrs Hooper. I think you're terrific.

MRS HOOPER. Somebody's got to put a bit o' meat into it. Is it the same tune?

PHYLLIS. Yes. Now. Ready? (*She raises one hand to beat time*)

(MRS HOOPER *takes a deep breath preparatory to singing;* MRS DEWSBURY *again interrupts*)

MRS DEWSBURY. A good job Miss Endling's gone.

PHYLLIS (*turning on her*) What? Why?

MRS DEWSBURY. Vegetarian.

PHYLLIS. What's that got to do with it?

MRS DEWSBURY. Not to mention teetotal.

MRS JONES (*fluttering*) Thank you, Mrs Dewsbury. I'm sure you're right, but I don't quite see . . .

MRS DEWSBURY. It says bring me flesh and bring me wine. She wouldn't hold with it.

MRS SMALLEY. Narrer.

MRS DEWSBURY. That's right—narrer. What's wrong with a bit o' flesh?

MRS HOOPER. *You* ought to know. You've put on enough!

MRS DEWSBURY. I don't get the exercise I did, and that's a fact.

MRS HOOPER. Not that I care for wine myself. Hooper
would have champagne—he said no marriage wasn't legal
without it. Twelve and six a bottle it was!

PHYLLIS. What did it taste like?

MRS HOOPER. I didn't have none. Legal or not, I said
beer I've been brought up on, and beer I'll have. And me
being the bride—*and* with experience, as you might say,
having had three . . .

PHYLLIS. Third time lucky, eh, Mrs Hooper?

MRS HOOPER (*jovially*) You'll find out, young woman.

PHYLLIS. I hope so. Early and often—that's my idea of
marriage.

MRS JONES (*shocked*) Oh, no, dear. After all—marriage,
you know . . .

MISS WARDLOW (*nervously intervening*) I don't want to in-
terrupt, of course—but if we *could* get on . . .

PHYLLIS. You're dead right, Miss Wardlow. I don't
know who started on marriage. A dreary subject, anyway.
Now, Mrs Hooper. You were going to give us the next bit.
All right, Mrs Dewsbury. Miss Endling having gone,
flesh and wine are in. *And* pine logs.

MRS DEWSBURY. If he'd gathered winter fuel, why did
they have to carry pine logs three miles?

PHYLLIS. Look, Mrs Dewsbury—I know it's nonsense, but
I didn't write it.

MRS JONES. Oh, no, dear. Not nonsense.

PHYLLIS (*cheerfully*) Absolute rot, if you ask me. But
most things are, aren't they? Why worry? Now, Mrs
Hooper. On the beat. One, two, three . . .

(MRS HOOPER *sings the next four lines, loudly and raucously*)

Now then—all together!

(*They sing the next four lines in chorus*)

There, Mrs Dewsbury. What do you say to that?

MRS DEWSBURY. I hope they was well wrapped up, that's
all.

MRS JONES. Oh, I'm sure they were.

MRS DEWSBURY. I'm not. You can't trust men. They've
no sense when it comes to wrapping up.

MRS HOOPER. 'Sright. If you had my lot you'd know. And who has to look after them when they catch cold? Me. And no thanks, neither.

MISS WARDLOW. I'm sure they're very grateful, really.

MRS HOOPER. Grateful! You'd think I'd *give* it them, the way they carry on.

MRS JONES. Now, Mrs Hooper—you know you spoil them all, including Mr Hooper.

MRS HOOPER. He was spoilt when I got him.

MRS SMALLEY. Not the only one.

MRS DEWSBURY. Get 'em young, *I* say.

PHYLLIS. Good Lord, no—they're the worst. But—yes, you're quite right, Miss Wardlow—this isn't getting anywhere. It's the page now.

HILDA. Me?

PHYLLIS. Just a minute. What about Mrs Dewsbury doing this bit? The page has just about had it, and she'll sound as though she was about to clock in at the golden gates.

MRS JONES. Oh, but we can't have *two* pages.

PHYLLIS. Who's to know? And it's time Mrs Dewsbury had a turn. Give it a trial, anyway. Now then, Mrs Dewsbury . . .

MRS DEWSBURY. I'll have a go with anybody. What's the words?

PHYLLIS. Verse four. Sire, the night is darker now.

MRS DEWSBURY. Clouded over like?

PHYLLIS. Yes. Come on before it begins to snow. Ready?

(MRS DEWSBURY *sings four lines, panting and wheezing, every two or three words*)

MRS DEWSBURY (*pleased*) How about it?

PHYLLIS. If that doesn't get sympathy, nothing will.

MRS HOOPER. Talk about a dying duck!

MRS DEWSBURY. It's me breath.

PHYLLIS. It was marvellous. Now, Mrs Hooper. This wants volume. Rattle the windows. There you are—mark my footsteps.

MRS SMALLEY. I don't see how you can warm snow by treading in it.

PHYLLIS. You can't. I told you it was nonsense. Come on, Mrs Hooper. Give it the works!

(MRS HOOPER *gives the next four lines full volume*)

Now the last verse. All together!

(*They give the last verse all they've got*)

(*Triumphantly*) There! And I'll bet old Wenceslas never got a show like that before. (*To Mrs Jones*) What do you say?

MRS JONES (*dubiously*) It certainly sounded different when the choir used to sing it.

PHYLLIS. I'll bet. Now we've got the idea what do we do next?

MRS JONES. Well—my intention was to sing it as we went through the village. So perhaps we ought to practise it walking.

MRS HOOPER. Running, more likely!

MRS DEWSBURY. Not me. I haven't run since I don't know when.

MISS WARDLOW. If we sing quietly perhaps no-one will notice.

PHYLLIS. No. We can't handicap Mrs Hooper. (*To Mrs Jones*) What do you say? Once through the village as a try-out?

MRS JONES (*flustered*) I hadn't intended—not quite so soon . . .

PHYLLIS. The sooner the better. Come on, everybody. Give the village a treat.

MRS JONES (*nervously*) Do you think the village will respond?

PHYLLIS. There is that danger, of course, but if we step on it we may get clear before they recover. Now—is everybody ready?

(*They all get up*)

MRS HOOPER. It's taking a chance, but I wasn't never one to avoid trouble.

MISS WARDLOW. Oh, do you think there will be?

PHYLLIS. We'll risk it. Remember the Christian martyrs. I'll lead the way, shall I? On the beat. One—two—three!

They leave the hall singing the first verse of the carol. It dies away in the distance.

MADE AND PRINTED IN GREAT BRITAIN BY
LATIMER TREND AND CO. LTD, PLYMOUTH
MADE IN ENGLAND